# Greater Than a Tourist Book Series
# Reviews from Readers

I think the series is wonderful and beneficial for tourists to get information before visiting the city.

-Seckin Zumbul, Izmir Turkey

I am a world traveler who has read many trip guides but this one really made a difference for me. I would call it a heartfelt creation of a local guide expert instead of just a guide.

-Susy, Isla Holbox, Mexico

New to the area like me, this is a must have!

 -Joe, Bloomington, USA

This is a good series that gets down to it when looking for things to do at your destination without having to read a novel for just a few ideas.

-Rachel, Monterey, USA

Good information to have to plan my trip to this destination.

-Pennie Farrell, Mexico

Great ideas for a port day.

-Mary Martin USA


Aptly titled, you won't just be a tourist after reading this book. You'll be greater than a tourist!

-Alan Warner, Grand Rapids, USA


Even though I only have three days to spend in San Miguel in an upcoming visit, I will use the author's suggestions to guide some of my time there. An easy read - with chapters named to guide me in directions I want to go.

 -Robert Catapano, USA


Great insights from a local perspective! Useful information and a very good value!

 -Sarah, USA


This series provides an in-depth experience through the eyes of a local. Reading these series will help you to travel the city in with confidence and it'll make your journey a unique one.

-Andrew Teoh, Ipoh, Malaysia

# GREATER THAN A TOURIST-SAN JOSE COSTA RICA

*50 Travel Tips from a Local*

Mieke Leenders

CZYK Publishing Since 2011.

Greater Than a Tourist

Lock Haven, PA
All rights reserved.

**ISBN:** 9781088482599

# >TOURIST

## 50 TRAVEL TIPS FROM A LOCAL

# BOOK DESCRIPTION

Are you excited about planning your next trip? Do you want to try something new? Would you like some guidance from a local? If you answered yes to any of these questions, then this Greater Than a Tourist book is for you. *Greater Than a Tourist-San Jose, Costa Rica* by Mieka Leenders gives you the inside scoop on San Jose. Most travel books tell you how to travel like a tourist. Although there is nothing wrong with that, as part of the Greater Than a Tourist series, this book will give you travel tips from someone who has lived at your next travel destination.

In these pages, you will discover advice that will help you throughout your stay. This book will not tell you exact addresses or store hours but instead will give you excitement and knowledge from a local that you may not find in other smaller print travel books.

Travel like a local. Slow down, stay in one place, and get to know the people and culture. By the time you finish this book, you will be eager and prepared to travel to your next destination.

Inside this travel guide book you will find:

- Insider tips from a local.

- Packing and planning list.

- List of travel questions to ask yourself or others while traveling.

- A place to write your travel bucket list.

# OUR STORY

Traveling is a passion of the Greater than a Tourist book series creator. Lisa studied abroad in college, and for their honeymoon Lisa and her husband toured Europe. During her travels to Malta, an older man tried to give her some advice based on his own experience living on the island since he was a young boy. She was not sure if she should talk to the stranger but was interested in his advice. When traveling to some places she was wary to talk to locals because she was afraid that they weren't being genuine. Through her travels, Lisa learned how much locals had to share with tourists. Lisa created the Greater Than a Tourist book series to help connect people with locals. A topic that locals are very passionate about sharing.

# TABLE OF CONTENTS

11. Visit Barrio Amon – district of the coffee barons
12. Learn all about the painted Oxcarts in Sarchi
13. Visit Volcano Irazu
14. Stroll through the haunted Duran Sanatorium
15. Cartago, city of legends and earthquakes
16. Head up to Poas, the weeping volcano
17. Take a Street Art walk
18. Mercado Central
19. Wander around the city center

EXPLORE SOME OPPORTUNITIES TO GIVE BACK

20. Spend a day planting trees
21. Visit Territorio de Zaguates
22. Look into volunteering opportunities

REMOTE HIKES IN AND AROUND SAN JOSE

23. Explore remote treasures with local touring agencies
24. Hike Cerro San Miguel and Pico Blanco
25. Hike to Piedra de Aserri, the rock housing a famous witch
26. Spot waterfalls
27. Mount Chirripo

FOOD CULTURE

28. Visit local Sodas
29. Try the artisanal ice cream – It tastes like Christmas

# DEDICATION

To all travelers who want to experience the soul of a place.

# ABOUT THE AUTHOR

Mieke Leenders is a writer and traveler from Belgium. After obtaining her master's degree in art history, she spent several years working as a freelance writer and hotel receptionist. In 2017, she decided to take the money she had saved and spend it on a year-long solo trip. After backpacking through Nepal and several countries in Latin America, she settled in Costa Rica. She is now further pursuing her passion for writing while also eagerly planning her next adventures. Next to travel and writing, Mieke is passionate about books, photography, animal rights, art and history.

# HOW TO USE THIS BOOK

The *Greater Than a Tourist* book series was written by someone who has lived in an area for over three months. The goal of this book is to help travelers either dream or experience different locations by providing opinions from a local. The author has made suggestions based on their own experiences. Please check before traveling to the area in case the suggested places are unavailable.

**Travel Advisories**: As a first step in planning any trip abroad, check the Travel Advisories for your intended destination.
https://travel.state.gov/content/travel/en/traveladvisories/traveladvisories.html

# FROM THE PUBLISHER

Traveling can be one of the most important parts of a person's life. The anticipation and memories that you have are some of the best. As a publisher of the Greater Than a Tourist, as well as the popular *50 Things to Know* book series, we strive to help you learn about new places, spark your imagination, and inspire you. Wherever you are and whatever you do I wish you safe, fun, and inspiring travel.

Lisa Rusczyk Ed. D.
CZYK Publishing

WELCOME TO
> TOURIST

I am very happy to be sharing 'my story so far' here in Costa Rica with you future travelers to the land of Pura Vida. I will be telling you all about my personal experiences, parts of Costa Rican culture I have fallen in love with and every practical tip I can think of to make your holiday run smoothly. From the must-sees and must-knows to the tucked away places you usually won't find in the glossy tourist guides, here are my 50 tips for travelers visiting San Jose, Costa Rica!

WELCOME TO SAN JOSE!

# 1. UNDERSTANDING PURA VIDA

Pura Vida means 'hi'. Pura Vida means 'bye'. Pura Vida means 'I am well' and Pura Vida means 'oh well, life goes on'. You will hear the words Pura Vida everywhere. When I first arrived in Costa Rica, I thought Pura Vida was nothing more than a phrase people used to greet one another and wish each other well. But it goes deeper than that.

Pura Vida, literally translated as Pure Life, is what actually defines the Tico way of life. It means to live worry-free, stress-free and allow the simple pleasures to rule your life. This intoxicating lifestyle seems both wonderful and alien to most of us and it is this that often turns tourists into regular visitors and sometimes even into residents.

I will expand on Pura Vida at the end of this book where I will also reveal my own path in finding my inner Pura Vida and what you can do to connect to yours.

# 2. FROM THE AIRPORT TO YOUR HOTEL

The Juan Santamaria International Airport is located in Alajuela, a mere 20 kilometers from downtown San Jose. While many of the more upscale hotels will offer shuttle services, there is also a bus stop right at the airport. The final stop is in downtown San Jose close to La Parque Merced, Tuasa. This is by far the cheapest way to travel. You can also take advantage of taxis or Ubers – I have provided more information on how to work with these below.

# 3. WHERE TO STAY

While known as a country where you can stay at luxury resorts and book all-inclusive packages to exotic destinations, you can also travel in a way that challenges you and brings you closer to the culture itself. San Jose has great options for low as well as high range budgets and here are the best choices for each of them.

## Budget options

A safe, a little bit on the fancy side, but backpacker-friendly district I used to visit before becoming a resident, was Gonzalez Lahmann, Barrio Escalante. This is a good place for those looking to be close to the action and also have interesting bars, restaurants an alternative movie theater and the national museum in the immediate area.

One of my favorite hostels was Costa Rica Guesthouse. They had affordable private rooms with a shared bathroom at a time I really needed a break from the chaotic dorm rooms I had been staying in for over a year. The guesthouse is quiet and charming with a simple but nice breakfast included in the price.

In the same area, the Garden Boutique Hostel and the Turtle Saving Hostel are known as the most highly rated hostels in San Jose. As the name suggests, if you stay at the latter hostel, 20% of your room rate will support the turtle conservation efforts in Costa Rica.

**The upscale experience**

I don't have personal experience with the more high end lodging options, but I have written on the subject many times back when I worked as travel writer in a local travel agency. If you don't mind staying a little bit further from downtown San Jose, Escazu (which for me will always be known as the City of Witches) is a favorite among luxury travelers as well as luxury residents. But if you are looking for a more upscale experience in the city center, both Hotel Grano Oro and Hotel Presidente came highly recommended by anyone who traveled with the agency I worked for.

# 4. PREPARE FOR THE PERHAPS UNEXPECTED WEATHER IN SAN JOSE

San Jose's weather is pretty pleasant all-year round and can be described as an 'eternal spring-like climate'. That being said, when visiting San Jose and surrounding areas, it is best to pack for hot as well as slightly chilly weather.

The dry season roughly runs from December to May. During this time, temperatures can range from anywhere between 20 and 30 degrees Celsius and drop significantly at night. The rainy season will still have its hot days and contrary to popular belief, showers are usually restricted to the afternoons.

I have always enjoyed traveling the country during rainy season more because prices tend to drop and there are far less tourists around. I had the best luck when visiting Manuel Antonio during rainy season and had sun all day with very few people in the park. Of course, sunny weather is never a given even in the mornings.

# 5. LOCAL CURRENCY

The local currency in Costa Rica is the Colon. While US dollars and credit cards are widely accepted in San Jose, it can't hurt to carry around some colones if you plan on visiting more remote areas and will be taking public transportation and taxis. But of course, it is also fun to learn to handle new money and some bills are so beautiful, you can even keep them as a souvenir (the 10,000 bill has a sloth on it!).

# CULTURE, HISTORY AND LEGENDS

I am very passionate about history and have spent many hours delving into Costa Rica's past. Your trip will gain real depth if you understand some of the factors that contributed to shaping the Costa Rica of today. One of these influencing factors, is contradiction. You will find high culture and street art inspired by European and North American artists as well as the passion and energy expressed by the everyday man and woman. And while modern culture is a lot more prevailing, you can also find a whisper of Costa Rica's Pre-Columbian past.

Here are some destinations in the city of San Jose where you can experience key moments in Costa Rican history, culture, folklore and legends.

# 6. VISIT THE PRE-COLUMBIAN GOLD MUSEUM

The Pre-Columbian Gold Museum, located at the very heart of the city, symbolizes power in the old world as well as the new. Gold was an element of true authority in Pre-Columbian Costa Rica, much like it still is now. Owned by the Central Bank of Costa Rica, you can see the country's first coin and the historical change printed money underwent as well as various golden artifacts and a replica of a Pre-Columbian grave that held 88 such objects.

Costa Rica's Pre-Columbian history isn't as present today as it is in other Latin American countries, but if you want to visit an extraordinary monument that will give you an insight in the architectural, ritualistic and social aspects of life in this time period, visit Guayabo!

# 7. TAKE A DAY TRIP TO GUAYABO NATIONAL MONUMENT

Guayabo will always be known as the place where I saw my first wild sloth. We had just parked our car when the security officer called us over and pointed up to the trees. It was a three-toed sloth with a baby and although very clear to me then, I would never have spotted it without help. It was the start of a great day which only got better when we walked through the paths exploring the archaeological remains.

Although less visited (and also less expensive), Guayabo holds the most important and well-preserved pre-Columbian findings. The remains point to a highly sophisticated and vibrant culture with ingenious aqueducts running through the town. You can see the foundation of various constructs from the Chief's strategically placed home to those of different classes as divided by construction type and location. You are also allowed a glimpse into the town's religious life a number of engraved rocks that are placed along the path showing the representation of reptiles and jaguars.

While visiting Guayabo, why not also explore some of the Orosi Valley? We took the alternative route back to San Jose and stopped off at the Iglesia de San Jose de Orosi, a charming little church built in 1743 and the oldest one in the country that is still in use. About 15 kilometers from Orosi, you will find the Ruins of Ujarras dating back to 1693. The beautiful gardens surrounding this landmark makes it a great place to sit and enjoy a quick snack. The rest of the ride back to San Jose will offer you stunning views of the valley including the Reventazon River (great for rafting), the 13,000 year old Cachi lake and the Cachi dam.

# 8. EXPLORE THE NATIONAL MUSEUM – THE SCARS OF THE PAST

While the Pre-Columbian Gold Museum symbolizes power, the National Museum's scarred walls represent a symbol for the irrevocable changes brought on by Costa Rica's most bloody chapter. The national museum is a must visit inside as well as out. I actually walked by this building several times without going in, only admiring it from the outside. Originally built as a military barracks in 1917, the outer wall is still a striking tribute to the transition from violence to peace. The bullets marking the wall

19

date back to the 1948 civil war, the conflict that also lead Costa Rica to being one of the few countries in the world without an army.

Inside, you can see permanent exhibitions on Costa Rica's history from geological, archaeological and colonial finds to modern history as well as a charming butterfly garden.

# 9. VISIT JUAN SANTAMARIA MUSEUM – DRUMMER BOY GONE NATIONAL HERO

One of the names that will sound instantly familiar to everyone, is Juan Santamaria. While most will recognize it as the name of the international airport in Alajuela, Juan Santamaria was a drummer boy whose actions proved pivotal in the Filibuster War of 1856. When William Walker and his army of mercenaries were pushed back into Nicaragua, they took shelter in a shed in Rivas. It was Juan Santamaria who volunteered to burn down the wooden construct and end the war, losing his own life in the process.

Juan Santamaria's museum is located in his hometown of Alajuela. The entrance is free of cost since the local people are proud to share the story of their local hero. Juan Santamaria also has a statue dedicated to him a short walk from the museum.

# 10. HOP INTO THE NATIONAL THEATER WHERE A SOPHISTICATED EUROPE MEETS RURAL COSTA RICA

When I first visited the national theater, I had been traveling for close to a year and the strong presence of European influences made me feel rather melancholy and home-sick. This place is worth a visit even when you are not catching a show. The lavishly decorated building first opened in 1897 with a performance of Goethe's Faust. The whole construction is an ode to the European arts with its neoclassical design and busts of Chopin, Beethoven and Calderon de la Barca.

Still maintaining a sense of Costa Rican identity, the ceiling mural designed by Italian artist J. Vila, is a striking representation of Costa Rica's rural life in this upscale, bourgeois setting.

The so called Allegory of Coffee and Bananas gives center stage to the country's agricultural triumphs.

21

The 19th and early 20th century were marked by a staggering economic growth due to banana and coffee production. It was thanks to this welfare as well as the taxes that were temporarily put on coffee, that financed this extravagant display. The scene is set in a highly romanticized setting that is something of an anomaly. While coffee is grown in the higher elevations, for example, the mural clearly shows a more exotic seaside setting.

Tip: From here you can take the San Jose City Tours leaving at 10 am every day. You can explore the city through the eyes of a local and disover San Jose's past. For example, did you know San Jose was not Costa Rica's first capital?

# 11. VISIT BARRIO AMON – DISTRICT OF THE COFFEE BARONS

Barrio Amon is a historical neighborhood just north of Morazan Parque. It is a true testament to the nouveau riche created by the wealth of the coffee industry and definitely worth an architectural stroll. The mansions inspire various time periods from Art Deco to Victorian styles of which many have been turned into hotels, restaurants or bars.

# 12. LEARN ALL ABOUT THE PAINTED OXCARTS IN SARCHI

Sarchi is a small town known for its production of traditional Costa Rican oxcarts. The initial designs in the 1800s were all about functionality, but the cart builders started to show a little bit more flash in the early 20th century. While the aristocracy was raving about the European art and large commissions were made in order to introduce more of its influences in San Jose, the cart builders turned themselves into artists in their own right. The carts slowly evolved into the uniquely colorful display of intricate designs they are today. You can visit two manufacturers where you can learn about the traditional way the carts were made and painted: Fabrica de Carretas Joaquin Chaverri and Fabrica de Carretas Eloy Alfaro.

# 13. VISIT VOLCANO IRAZU

Irazu can be visited independently as well as in tour, but I would recommend you go on your own. It is so easy to arrange it yourself and you will save quite a few bucks. Buses leave close to the national theater at 8am every morning. Start queuing for the bus as early as possible and make sure you are one of the first to arrive because once full, those in the back of the line will have to find another way to get there. Should you be one of the unfortunate ones, you can take the one to Cartago and make your way up to Irazu from there where buses to the volcano leave from the Cartago ruins.

We were some of the last to make it on the bus from San Jose which was packed, mainly with local families enjoying a weekend trip. The bus takes you all the way up to the volcano. This is quite different from my usual off the road hiking experiences, but interesting in its way and a great option for those who are less able to climb steep slopes or those who travel in a wheelchair.

Our steady rise up the Irazu slopes was halted by a long line of cars queuing to the entrance. The driver said we could walk ahead if we wanted since the entrance was only about 2k away, so we decided to go with that. Once at the entrance, however, we learned that you could only enter the park in a vehicle. Luckily, we were able to join a lovely family in theirs just a couple of cars removed from the entrance.

Irazu is a stunning volcano which only allows you top peer through its cloud deck on occasion. You can walk from the summit at 3432 meters (you can park your car here) and explore the various craters. It is an easy walk that doesn't take you no more than 1-1.5 hours to make your way slowly throughout the park.

Irazu has had quite a thunderous past which has inspired two beautiful legends in the city of Cartago and created the most haunted location in Costa Rica.

# 14. STROLL THROUGH THE HAUNTED DURAN SANATORIUM

On your way back down from Irazu, definitely stop off at the Duran Sanatorium. This is an excellent destination for history buffs, photographers and those who enjoy a good ghost story. The Duran Sanatorium has the honor of being the most haunted location in the whole country. First built in the early 19-hundreds as a tuberculosis hospital, Duran has had several other lives as a sanctuary for the mentally ill, an orphanage and a prison. I love my horror movies and I can't count the amount of films inspired by a setting that has just one of these stories tied to it, let alone 4.

After Irazu's temperamental nature caused irreparable structural damage, the sanatorium fell out of use and slowly became the urban explorer's dream it is today.

# 15. CARTAGO, CITY OF LEGENDS AND EARTHQUAKES

When I visited Cartago it was rainy, dark and an eerie Brontë-esque glow fell over the city. This created the perfect atmosphere for my visit to the church ruins and the basilica of Cartago.

The Basílica de Nuestra Señora de Los Angeles (Our Lady of the Angels) and the Santiago Apóstol Parish Ruins, combine Costa Rica's passion for the catholic faith with its belief in the symbolic power of nature's erratic moods.

The basilica's legend talks of a peasant girl who found a small statue of the virgin Mary cradling a baby Jesus on a rock. She took the statue home but found that it was gone the next day, back on the rock, where it kept reappearing even when later attempts were made to remove the figure. Earthquakes plagued the construction of the basilica until they moved the site to the location where the statue was discovered.

Here, they were able to finish building the basilica which has now been restored in a colonial style mixed with a Neo-Byzantine flair.

Today, the basilica remains a popular pilgrimage site and a large group of believers, young and old, still make their way to the alter on their knees. On your visit, make sure to also take a sip of the healing source of water that springs next to the church.

After a short walk from the basilica, you will encounter the Santiago Apóstol Parish Ruins that inspired a more disturbing legend. The story goes that two brothers, one a priest and one a likable layabout, had their eye on the same woman. When the woman chose the idle brother, the priest was driven mad by jealousy. When his brother visited the church on New Year's Eve of 1577, the priest killed him in a fit of fury. As a form of penance, the priest built a church for the city which was continuously destroyed by earthquakes until construction was finally halted in 1910.

These legends are a magnificent testament to how the Costa Rican people live closer to nature. Eruptions and earthquakes are more than just a natural way, but a sign and a way for nature to communicate its will.

# 16. HEAD UP TO POAS, THE WEEPING VOLCANO

I will be honest... While this is a stunning destination, I don't want to tell you about the volcano itself, but rather about its beautiful origin story now known as the most moving legend in Costa Rica. According to the story, a tribal girl living on Poas' slopes befriended a Rualdo bird. When Poas showed alarming signs, the girls' father, a powerful shaman, visited the volcano in order to try and mediate some form of peace and prevent the destruction of his village. When learning this was impossible, the only solution he saw was to sacrifice his daughter to the volcano.

Despite her pleas for mercy, the girl was dragged to the fiery mound. It was at this moment that the Rualdo bird appeared and offered the volcano its song in exchange for the girl's life. Poas was so moved by the sheer beauty of the song, it wept and its tears created the silvery blue lake we still see today.

# 17. TAKE A STREET ART WALK

Street art is the visual poetry of a city. It gives you a real insight into what people think and feel beyond the borders of conventional culture. San Jose has some incredible areas known for its urban art and it is well worth exploring.

From San Pedro and Calle de la Amargura and de Montes de Oca to other neighborhoods such as Otoya, Amón, La California and Escalante, Aranjuez, Dent, … Street art is everywhere. I have always happened upon it by accident while walking or taking the bus, but I have heard of a tour organized by a project called Costa Rica en la Pared (Costa Rica on the wall). They take you on the so called Urban Art Tour and delve into San Jose's artistic underground as well as the social and political wars that are colorfully retold on the city walls.

# 18. MERCADO CENTRAL

While a stroll through downtown San Jose might not give you the instant impression of being in Costa Rica, a visit to the Mercado Central will. As soon as you walk into this indoor market, your senses will instantly be assaulted by the pungent scent of fish and spices, a colorful display of flowers and locally grown fruits and vegetables. In-between the stalls, you will find the occasional shop selling cooking equipment as well as restaurants serving local dishes with the waitresses loudly citing daily specials.

Even when you don't plan on purchasing anything, a wander through the central market will give you a real feel for the vibrant energy that lays at the foundation of Costa Rican culture.

# 19. WANDER AROUND THE CITY CENTER

One of my favorite things to do when visiting a new city, is simply wandering around and see what I come across. San Jose is a lively place and they are always looking to express their identity in different ways. When I was taking a walk through town last April, they had just launched a new exhibition by local sculptor Jorge Jimenez Deredia. His sculptures were placed all across the center exploring the themes of motherhood, birth and fertility. Although over by now, this exhibition was only one of the many city projects set up throughout the year.

# EXPLORE SOME OPPORTUNITIES TO GIVE BACK

# 20. SPEND A DAY PLANTING TREES

Costa Rica is one of the countries that has communicated highly ambitious goals in regards to its environmental policy. Since tourism can be a great strain on a country, you can offset the carbon emissions of your flights and on-land transportation by planting trees. There are several such initiatives across the country but one of the closest to San Jose as well as the most famous, is organized by Kids Saving the Rainforest.

# 21. VISIT TERRITORIO DE ZAGUATES

Zaguates has to be my favorite destination I haven't visited yet. Not for lack of trying, though. As I am writing this, the famous dog sanctuary is closed for renovations. But I can assure you that as soon as it opens, I will be first in line.

Territorio de Zaguates means Land of the Strays and is home to over 1300 dogs looking for a home. While the situation in Costa Rica has vastly improved for companion animals since the Animal Welfare Bill of 2017, just like in every country, there are still many dogs that need love and attention. You can support Zaguates by donating money or donating in kind. They have a list of materials they need on the website.

# 22. LOOK INTO VOLUNTEERING OPPORTUNITIES

Volunteering is a great way to learn more about local initiatives, culture, and what challenges Costa Rica is facing. While just volunteering during your trip is a worthy pass-time, it would be great for you to select a program you are very passionate about and continue contributing even after your travels and form a more sustainable relationship with the organization. Many choose to contribute further by adopting a sloth or turtle through organizations such as the above mentioned Kids Saving the Rainforest and the Corcovado Foundation or help raise funds for projects.

If you would like to contribute to another type of organization, Costa Rica also has many social projects supporting local children as well as adults such as Lifting Hands and Seeds of Hope. One of the ways to help is by researching a project called Pack for a Purpose. They have initiatives set up in various countries where charitable organizations post an updated list of supplies they need to keep their good work going.

## REMOTE HIKES IN AND AROUND SAN JOSE

If you are looking for tips from a local, you are no doubt wanting to hear about more than just Pacuare, Monteverde, Manuel Antonio, and so on... Here are a list of tips and destinations that most tourists receive little to no information about.

## 23. EXPLORE REMOTE TREASURES WITH LOCAL TOURING AGENCIES

If you can handle yourself in Spanish and want to experience something beyond the big touring agencies, why not go local? You will discover places you might never have even heard of, spruce up your Spanish, spend time traveling with locals and save quite a bit of money.

All arrangements are made through Facebook, where they advertise a new adventure every weekend. The best ones you can travel with are:

Chirripó Mountain Adventures (top of the list!)

Sitios Ticos

Poás Rutas

Alajueliteños a Pata (run by my husband's cousin)

All tours will mention what the difficulty level is, what is included in the price and what you need to bring yourself. Make sure to check this in detail because not all agencies provide meals.

Once you selected a tour you'd like to go on, you will be asked to pay by bank transfer around 3 days prior to the hike. Most agencies work with common Costa Rican banks like Banco Nacional de Costa Rica, Banco de Costa Rica and BAC (private), but since you will most likely not have a local bank account yourself, you can make the transfer in cash. Simply visit the bank the agency is affiliated with, hand over their account information and the money. Make sure to ask for a receipt to show your tour guide.

TIP: If you are making a transfer through Banco Nacional de Costa Rica or Banco de Costa Rica, start queuing close to opening time in the morning. These are the most popular banks and the lines can get very long.

# 24. HIKE CERRO SAN MIGUEL AND PICO BLANCO

This is the kind of trip the above mentioned agencies are likely to take you on. Cerro San Miguel is a favorite hike among locals that offers breathtaking views of San Jose on one side, and the valley on the other. The 2035 meter top is market by a giant, metal cross that lights up at night, also making this hike a popular pilgrimage route. The presence of the cross and dedication to Saint Micheal has earned Cerro San Miguel the local nickname of La Cruz. The hike leaves from Llano Alajuelita but if you would like to take an alternative route back to San Jose, you can head down the other way and follow the river to Escazu.

While the hike to Cerro San Miguel is of moderate intensity, the 2271 meter Pico Blanco is a more stertorous day hike best reserved for those with good fitness levels. You will start and end your hike in San Antonio de Escazú. Make sure to visit this mountain with a guide since the thick, humid forests you pass through can obscure the sometimes already hard to spot trail. While the lower levels of the forest can be hot and humid, be prepared for a chilly wind at the top! Actually, bring a light jacket for La Cruz as well.

## 25. HIKE TO PIEDRA DE ASERRI, THE ROCK HOUSING A FAMOUS WITCH

This rock ties in with another one of San Jose's local legends. It is said that this rock was once home to a witch called Zarate. Although never confirmed by geological studies, the door to the rock is said to lead to tunnels that go back all the way to Escazu. I have referred to Escazu briefly as the City of Witches and its emblem still features the symbol of a witch on a broom. In the 1600s, Escazu was home to a group of midwives providing herbal treatments for the locals. While the women's cures were denounced as fraudulent by the 19th century and gave birth to various terrifying legends, Costa Rica never took cruel measures against these healers like other parts of the world and merely let the women off with a fine and restraining order.

You can start this not too demanding hike at the Poás de Aserrí bus stop and climb up through fields, farms and coffee plantations until you reach the giant rock offering a wonderful view.

# 26. SPOT WATERFALLS

Costa Rica has so many waterfalls, the only difficulty is in choosing which ones to visit. Local agencies will make the occasional trip to a remote waterfall evaded by the big touring agencies, but I want to make special mention of Los Chorros in Grecia, Alajuela, and Sendero Ecologico Finca San Gerardo, San Ramon. I have not visited these myself yet because I don't have a car and have been told you need one (4 wheel drive essential), but one of my coworkers here in Costa Rica is a real waterfall hunter and loved these off-the-road gems that are generally only visited by locals. With tourist not yet swarming these destinations, Costa Ricans take full advantage of enjoying a refreshing swim during the weekends and it can get pretty busy starting noon. So if you can, visit during week.

# 27. MOUNT CHIRRIPO

I absolutely love mountains and Chirripo is the tallest one in Costa Rica, standing proudly at 3820 meters (12, 532 feet). Chirripo is not exactly unknown but it is rarely on the list of first time travelers to Costa Rica since it doesn't seem to communicate the typical Costa Rica traits of rainforests and beaches that people want to scratch off their list first. But what it lacks in sandy shores, it more than makes up for in spectacular biodiversity as you hike from pastures and rainforests all the way up to a tundra climate. This hike will be more than worth your while.

Mount Chirripo is between 3 and 4 hours south of the city and many touring agencies, including the above mentioned local ones, offer tours starting from San Jose. Hiking up this beast will be a challenge and I would recommend you acclimatize before embarking on this journey. San Jose has an altitude of 1170 meters so that is a good place to start. If you live in a region with a lower altitude, take a while to explore other parts of San Jose and be active before going on your hike. Also make sure to apply for the mandatory permit!

# FOOD CULTURE

# 28. VISIT LOCAL SODAS

A soda is a small, local restaurant where traditional dishes are served. Costa Rica's national dish is the Gallo Pinto, a breakfast made of a mixture of rice and beans, vegetables and spices. I used to visit loads of Sodas in the past because for the first couple of months I lived in a small room that had no kitchen. But now I have a kitchen and can also make a delicious Gallo Pinto, which I do practically every day now.

The traditional lunch is called a Casado, which consists of rice and beans, a salad, fried plantains and chicken or beef. You might have already guessed from reading about these dishes, that it is quite easy to be a vegetarian in Costa Rica. I am one myself and while it has proven difficult (though not impossible) in some cultures, it is relatively easy here. If you are a vegetarian too it is best to ask how they cook their beans. Some people cook them in a meaty broth.

Sodas are a must if you want to experience local culture and the dishes are usually very cheap yet delicious. One of the best sodas I can recommend in the city center, is El Burro Loco.

# 29. TRY THE ARTISANAL ICE CREAM – IT TASTES LIKE CHRISTMAS

I actually first visited San Jose when I was on my way to Bolivia. I was going to take the bus from San Jose to Panama the next day and travel by plane from there. My then boyfriend and now husband Allan went with me to San Jose and was very keen to take me to the Mercado Central where he wanted me to try the artisanal ice cream they served there. It was to him one of the most important things you had to do when visiting San Jose.

I am not the biggest ice cream fan but I loved that one. The strong presence of cloves and cinnamon reminded me of some of the German Christmas treats I would munch on every December. And every other month I could find them as well.

# 30. FARMER'S MARKETS

There are many markets in and around San Jose that are worth a visit if you plan on cooking or if you just want to learn about the local products, especially the fruit. You can engage in a conversation about food and sample some of the produce.

Here is a list of the most visited farmer's markets in San Jose.

Verde de Aranjuez:

Saturdays from 7am to 12.30pm

Feria  Verde de Colon:

Tuesdays  from 1pm to 7pm

Feria Organica el Trueque:

Saturdays from 5am to 12pm

Mercado  Natural de Curridabat:

Sundays from 8am to 2pm. This one is known as a type of        "hipster market" where they also give yoga classes and massages.   A  bit  more  expensive than the other ones.

La  Feria en Zapote:

Sundays  from 7am to 1pm

Feria de Atenas:

Fridays from 5am to 12pm

# GOING OUT

Ticos love a good party as well as a good dinner and you will never get bored at night (except during Holy Week when everyone is at the beach!). There a many different places to explore but here are some of the most iconic ones as well as some favorites of mine.

# 31. CATCH A MOVIE AT CINEMA MAGALY

There are many movie theaters in San Jose and almost all of them show the movie in the original language with Spanish subtitles, but this one is for the type of person who enjoys watching the alternative movies. The first movie I saw here, was Wes Anderson's Isle of Dogs. They show the kind of films that are whimsical and offbeat, like Anderson's movies, but also those with a strong political or social message.

# 32. GO TO BARRIO ESCALANTE – A GASTRONOMIC DELIGHT

Barrio Escalante is close to the above mentioned movie theater and is known for its artisanal flavors and experimental gastronomy with national as well as international flavors. You will pay a penny more at most places but they are definitely worth it. Try some delicious beers from micro-breweries, eat alcoholic ice cream, or just wander the streets during one of the street festivals they often have during the weekends.

# 33. BARRIO CALIFORNIA AND LA CALLE DE LA AMARGURA, THE ROWDIER CROWDS

First tip, if you plan on going out in these districts, bring as little as possible. Mugging is not unusual especially in La Calle de la Amargura, which translates as The Street of Bitterness. I realize I am not exactly selling you on these places right now but they have their charm. This is the type of place you want to visit if you want to party with students and other young crowds and enjoy cheap drinks and cheap food.

Barrio California is definitely the safer (and cleaner) of the two and more poplar with tourists and expatsl.

You can go to the so-called Street of Bitterness if you feel like experiencing the real college party scene, but only go in group and get an Uber back to your hotel rather than walking.

## 34. MIRADOR RESTAURANTS, DINNER AND A VIEW

Let's not forget that San Jose is located in a valley surrounded by volcanoes and that there are plenty of places where you can enjoy a good dinner as well as a view. Restaurant Tiquicia is a pretty touristy Mirador restaurant in Alajuela where they also perform dance shows. If you prefer the kind of place where you will rarely see tourists, go to Restaurante Italiano y Mirador Valle Azul in Alajuelita. A little lower down the road you will find Restaurante Mirador America, but this place is better if you just plan on enjoying a beer because the food is better in the first restaurant.

## 35. GENERAL TIPS FOR GOING OUT IN COSTA RICA

- Safety first, travel back to your hotel with Uber. While generally safe, you are a tourist and you stand out.

- Try some of the local alcoholic beverages! The national beers are Imperial and Pilsen. Pilsen is the stronger of the two. Cacique is the national spirit, but I am not very fond of it unless mixed.

- You don't have to tip in Costa Rica since all services are included in the bill. I only tip if I really appreciated someone's services.

# TRANSPORTATION

# 36. PUBLIC BUSES

I often take the public buses in San Jose because they are very cheap and have fairly regular driving times (although no specific times are posted). You can get from one side of the city to another for less than one dollar. The line and destination is always indicated on the front of the bus but to avoid getting lost, ask the driver if he will stop close to your destination.

There are several lines that take you by the most important destinations in the city center like Sabana Cemeterio 1 and 2 and Sabana Estadio. There is also a Periferica but this line is notoriously slow.

Remember these tips when taking the public bus in San Jose:

- Join the line at the bus stop. You will notice that locals instinctively form a line at the stop and it is considered good manners to stick to that without pushing and shoving.

- Only pay cash and in Colones. Other currency will not be accepted.

- Use this opportunity to get rid of your coins and try to avoid paying with 10,000 Colones bills and higher.

- If you have to queue, don't stand between the bars but rather wait outside the doors until you can walk straight up to the driver. The bars are counters that can cause miscounting if you stand between them for longer than one second. Some drivers can get angry if this happens.

- Buses can get pretty full and full buses are a breeding ground for pickpockets. Make sure you keep your belongings close to you.

- If you can, avoid using the handicapped seats (indicated by the wheelchair sign and a different color). If the bus is otherwise full, keep an eye out for handicapped people or mothers with small children getting on the bus so you can offer them your seat.

- For most of us, it is common to offer your seat to senior citizens. In Costa Rica the same unspoken rule applies even though most of the time, men offer their seat to women. It is considered kind and appropriate to do the same and offer your seat at least to senior citizens.

- Make sure you locate the stop button or cord when getting on the bus. Most buses have the cord but for the ones who don't, it is possible the button is pretty far removed from your seat.

# 37. TRAINS

I have never actually taken a train in Costa Rica, but from San Jose you can visit Heredia, Cartago Belen, Curridabat and Pavas by train. The major train stop is very centrally located close to the Parque Central. You can visit the Tren Urbano de Costa Rica website to check on travel times and rates: http://www.trenurbano.co.cr/horario_tren_urbano.asp x

# 38. TAXI VS UBER

The official taxis are red with a yellow triangle. Make sure you first check if the taxi has a running meter, this is obligatory, and request that they turn it on. Also, always have cash on hand since most taxis will not accept payments by card (If you want to ask if they do accept card say "se acepta tarjeta?").

While taking a taxi is generally safe, I would recommend using an Uber instead. Taxi drivers have a good eye for newbies and have been known to take advantage of it. When I first arrived in San Jose, I had it happen that a taxi driver tried to rip me off by taking an alternative route stating bad road conditions or a similar excuse and then overcharging. I have since heard many more stories like this.

Uber, on the other hand, is not only a lot cheaper but the drivers are also tied to their navigation app, basing possible detours only on heavy traffic which you can confirm on the app itself.

One thing Uber drivers appreciate is that you join them in the front seat so it doesn't immediately seem like a paid ride. Taxi drivers are not particularly happy about Uber stealing their work and they have been known to vandalize the cars and threaten the drivers.

For this reason, I usually ask for an Uber a little while away from the taxi drivers, memorize the license plate and the direction the Uber will be coming from so I don't stare at my phone all the time (also good to prevent your phone from being stolen!) and greet the driver like a friend.

# 39. DRIVING IN SAN JOSE

If you are planning on renting a car, there are a couple of things you should know about driving in San Jose. Here is a list of my most important tips for you!

- Waze is considered the best navigation app for Costa Rica. Every local uses it.

- In Costa Rica, you drive on the right side of the road.

- The road signs read in kilometers. The speed limit on the highways is 90 km/hour.

- The drivers license obtained in your home country is perfectly fine for driving in Costa Rica.

- There are traffic rules in Costa Rica, but locals usually don't stick to them. Be vigilant at all times.

- If you want to change a lane, don't simply use your blinkers and move. Most drivers will not pay attention to it. Make eye-contact and wait for the other driver to gesture you can move in front of them. Most drivers honk their horn as a 'thank you' in response. In fact, they honk on almost every occasion so feel free to join in on the honking culture.

- Road conditions are not always great and you should make sure to drive carefully to avoid damaging the car in potholes. Be mindful of the movements of other drivers and when they maneuver, do the same. Also, keep an eye on the gutters when turning in the smaller roads. They can be very deep and wide because they are built to get rid of the water faster in case of storms.

- If you get stuck behind a big truck on a small road, they will use their left blinker to communicate it is safe to pass them by. But I recommend you still confirm that for yourself.

- Keep an eye out for motorcycles and scooters! There are many of them about and they can shoot out from any direction.

- Always add around 30 minutes of travel time to whatever your navigation app says, especially when driving out of the city. These apps usually don't account for small, steep mountain roads.

# 40. WALKING

I love walking around town because it is the best way to discover new things and it is good exercise (there are quite a few hills in San Jose!). My tips for walking in San Jose:

- If you need to ask directions, know that there is no traditional address system in Costa Rica. Remembering landmarks is the best way to not get lost and to understand the directions locals will give you.

- You can of course also use the app on your phone for directions, but keep in mind that phone theft is very common here. It is better to study the map and keep your phone safe than it is to hold it.

- If a car stops for you when crossing the road, double-check behind that car because many drivers will pass by without paying much attention to why a car stopped. A lot of accidents happen this way.

- Just like with driving, here too it is important to cross the road only after making eye-contact with the driver and waiting for them to confirm you can cross. Sometimes a car might slow down not because they saw you, but because they are texting while driving (this happens a lot!).

- Cars can appear from every small street at high speed so keep an eye out at all times.

- Pay extra attention to motorcycles. Like in most other countries, they will move swiftly through traffic and pass cars by.

- Wear comfortable shoes when walking around San Jose. Sometimes there is no sidewalk and there can be holes in the road, especially outside of the metropolitan area.

- Always keep your belongings close!

# 41. RIDING A BIKE

I am a keen cyclist and have used my bike in many places in the country, but not yet in San Jose. While riding a bike in San Jose is possible, it can also be pretty dangerous. Make sure to take the following tips into account!

- There is no real infrastructure provided for cyclists so you will be sharing the road with drivers. Be vigilant at all times! While the same is true in many medieval cities in my native Belgium (like Gent where I lived for several years), the drivers in San Jose are not conditioned to driving with cyclists on the road since not many people travel this way. This is very different from Gent where there are often more cyclists than drivers on the road.

- Always wear a reflective vest and helmet.

- Even when just hopping into a shop for a short period of time, use a bike lock.

# SHOPPING

# 42. SUPERMARKETS

While traveling, I usually rented a bed in a hostel that also had a shared kitchen. Shopping in local supermarkets is a great way to practice your Spanish as well as save a whole lot of money. Here is a list of some of the most common supermarkets in San Jose:

- Pali and Maxipali are the cheapest grocery stores in the country.

- MegaSuper is very common and a tiny bit more expensive.

- MasxMenos is the shopping option with an average price range that also has a decent selection of important products.

- You will find even more imported goods in Perimercado and especially Automercado, but also note that these supermarkets are on the expensive side.

- Fresh Market and AM-PM are pretty popular with some of my Expat friends, but in all honesty they are simply overpriced convenient stores and I never visit them for that reason. They are just the "hip" kind of places to go to.

- Wal-Mart – Yep, they exists here and offer local products as well as imported ones.

- The so called Chinos can be found all over town. They are pretty affordable, small supermarkets run by Chinese families (hence the name).

You can of course also visit the farmer's markets! I expanded on the markets in San Jose in the Food Culture section.

# 43. MALLS

If you need to get some quick clothing shopping done to replace lost or damaged items, you will be able to find clothing stores scattered all over the city. In addition to that, you also have an easy connection to the malls where next to clothing you will find food courts, gyms, movie theaters, electronics, book stores, banks, opticians, pharmacies, banks, etc... I am not a big fan of malls so I can give you a list but I can't tell you which ones are the best:

- Mall San Pedro (Only place I have visited so far and just to get a simple tattoo done without a long waiting list and queue at the Banco Nacional. Nice and laid-back vibe and a high amount of sex shops, weirdly)

- Multiplaza Escazu (I am told this one is very close to US culture but also very expensive)

- Plaza del Este (Curridabat. Wait, I have been to this one too! But only to go to the movies. It was literally the only theater that had decent seats left for Endgame.)

- Terramall (Tres Rios)

- Plaza Lincoln (Moravia)

- City Mall (Alajuela)

- Paseo Metrolpoli (Cartago)

- Paseo de las Flores (Heredia)

- Oxigeno (Heredia)

# 44. SOUVENIRS

If you plan on visiting the above mentioned Sarchi, you can pick up a colorful little souvenir from one of the shops in town as well as the manufacturers themselves. Close to Sarchi, you can take a tour of the Doka Estate and pick up a souvenir with different historical value: coffee. While I haven't focused on coffee as much, there are plenty of tours you can take and Doka offers one of the most famous ones.

You might prefer the kitschy kind of souvenirs and shop for clothes and caps imprinted with Pura Vida (I have a blue t-shirt with a big sloth on it), colorful paintings of poison dart frogs, hammocks, … Then you will probably love the Mercado Municipal de Artesanías, open from 8 am to 7 pm every day.

If you can afford to spend a little bit more on a souvenir and want something more unique, visit the charming Biesanz Woodworks in Escazu. Barry Biesanz is a celebrated woodcarver who draws inspiration form pre-Columbian techniques. While the pieces are expensive and a small carving can cost around 50 USD, it will most definitely be a special way to commemorate your trip to Costa Rica.

# IN CASE OF ILLNESS

Call 911 in case of emergency

Costa Rica has excellent clinics and hospitals and you will not have a problem getting the appropriate care. Some general tips are to always bring your passport (you do not need to be a resident to get treated here) with you as well as a list of medical conditions you have and medications you are taking right now. Lines can get very, very long and waiting time can be bad in some cases so make sure to state clearly if you are suffering from asthma, high blood pressure, diabetes, are pregnant or over 65 years old, because then you will be receive preferential treatment. Also note that most hospitals will have at least some staff that speaks English, so don't worry if you feel your Spanish is not good enough to describe the issues you are having.

# 45. LOCAL PHARMACIES

You can purchase most medicine for which you need a prescription back home, over the counter here in Costa Rica. All you have to do is either request the specific medicine or describe your symptoms. The concept of a GP doesn't really exist here, but a lot of

57

pharmacies have a doctor present. If you need to, you can request to see the doctor for a consultation, but be prepared to wait in line.

# 46. DOCTORS WITHOUT BORDERS AND OTHER CLINICS

For non-emergencies, clinics are the better option for you. Private clinics like Clinica Biblica have an excellent reputation and still don't break the bank for a regular visit. One of my friends has stated Doctors without Borders as one of the best options for those without insurance (get insurance, though). She went there with a throat infection and only had to wait a couple of minutes for treatment and paid very little. It is the kind of clinic that is intended for low-income families in the area.

# 47. HOSPITALS

Private hospitals (like Cime) will cost more, but you will get faster service. That being said, make sure to check what your insurance covers exactly because private hospitals are often part of primary insurance plans.

While the actual treatment is top notch in both private and public hospitals, I have heard horror stories about the waiting time in the public ones. If you had an accident or an injury that involves blood, you will be fine. But with any type of internal distress that doesn't result in obvious wounds for which you still want treatment right now, you are better off with the private hospitals because you will get far more efficient service.

## SAFETY IN COSTA RICA

## 48. BEWARE OF MUGGERS AND PETTY THEFT

Let it first be said that yes, Costa Rica is a safe place for tourists. Crime rates are mainly tied to petty theft and mugging. I have been mugged myself once in San Jose but this was near my previous home in a very residential / urban area. This is where tourists generally don't go and where mugging rates are higher.

If a mugging does occur, immediately hand over your belongs. It is commonly known that muggers usually only resort to violence if they have to. During my travels, I have developed the habit of carrying around a fake wallet and an old phone to immediately hand over to muggers without much of a loss. More precious things I would keep in a money belt under my clothes. I recommend you do the same.

While mugging is higher in residential areas, petty theft is more common at the big tourist attractions. Make sure to always keep an eye on your things and always keep valuables either in a hotel safe or on your person and don't keep them in open pockets.

Lastly, you should always be careful when leaving the bus at the big terminals (for example the ones leaving for Guanacaste) or a more remote bus stop. Make sure all of your belongings are in place before leaving the bus. Many muggers take advantage of people still fiddling with their things after getting off the bus. You should also remain aware in the areas around the terminals. In fact, it is best to arrive and leave directly by Uber and avoid walking in these areas altogether.

# 49. INSECTS, WILDLIFE AND NATURAL DISASTER

Animals

When it comes to wildlife, always stick to the following rules. Do not touch, tease or feed the animals and do not take photos with a flash. Refrain from grabbing hold of trees or other flora randomly without consulting your guide and know that it is now forbidden to pose for a photo with wildlife in Costa Rica - this includes sport-fishing.

If you are planning a rain forest hike, equip yourself with bug spray and wear long pants and closed shoes. If you are spending the night at the rain forest or even at the beach, make sure to check your shoes for spiders or scorpions. Do the same if you are camping in remote areas and make use of outside showers and toilets.

I read that the scorpions here in Costa Rica are not dangerous unless you are allergic to them (which you sadly won't know until you get stung so avoid this at all cost). I have been stung twice so far and had no pain, swelling or other effects from it other than an "oh my god!" because they stung me in my sleep when I rolled over on them. So oh yes... Use mosquito nets too which I stupidly didn't while also sleeping on a mattress on the floor rather than an elevated platform. You are right, I deserved to be stung.

Earthquakes

As far as natural disasters go, mild earthquakes are very common in San Jose but I have also experienced one bigger earthquake that made my bed shake violently and my closet migrate halfway across the room.

The most important tip is, you guessed it, to stay calm. The recommended steps to take in case of an earthquake are to DROP to the ground and take COVER under a sturdy piece of furniture where you can HOLD on to something. If you can't take cover underneath a piece of furniture, crouch in a corner with your arms over your head.

To be honest, I didn't do any of these things during my first big earthquake and just sat up, dazed, still half-dreaming that my bed took off flying. The earthquake was over before I could wake up properly but luckily, there was no severe damage.

# 50. USE COMMON SENSE

Common sense will always be your friend. When traveling, you should simply apply the same rules you do at home and know which areas to avoid, keep an eye on your belongings and listen to the advice given by your guides. If you keep the above mentioned tips in mind, there is no reason for you to have anything but a safe and comfortable trip.

# BONUS TIPS: FIND YOUR INNER PURA VIDA

## LEARN TO DANCE

Latin dance is all about surrendering yourself to the rhythm and releasing your inhibitions. Where dance is about releasing your physical inhibitions, Pura Vida is, in a sense, about releasing your mental inhibitions. And you'd be surprised how much dance can help you with that. When conquering a new type of dance and movement, you may just feel more inclined towards doing the same for your mindset. Whether it is a newly found confidence or just the thrill of being in new surroundings, just see where it takes you.

# MASTER SOME TICO SPANISH

You'd feel and sound far more relaxed when you can break free from some of the more traditional Spanish sayings, so here are 10 examples of Tico slang (other than Pura Vida) to get you going.

- Tico / Tica: I have mentioned the word Tico before without actually saying what it means. Tico is the local slang for a Costarican man while Tica is the same for a woman.

- Mae: the Tico word for "dude"

- Chepe: this is a nickname used for the city of San Jose. Chepe is technically a slang word for the name 'Jose', so this is a nicknames for a person applied to the city.

- Tuanis: Cool

- Que chiva: How great, how cool

- Por dicha: An expression of relief similar to 'Thank God'

- Chunches: Things of Stuff

- Zarpe: Final round of drinks

- Que camote: How crazy

- Al Chile: You're kidding!

# PRACTICE PATIENCE AND JUST RELAX

"This is the life", Allan would say every time we'd slump back in a lounge chair at a beach-front bar after a day of hiking and exploring. As a Tico, Allan has fully mastered the art of Pura Vida. I am, in all honesty, still an apprentice.

As a Belgian raised by a mother who is strongly shaped by German standards, I have been taught to like efficiency, privacy, punctuality and candidness … In addition to that, I am a pretty cynical person by nature. Although I have loosened up quite a bit after being exposed to different cultures and people during my life as well as my travels, I am still far from Pura Vida.

The good part about living in as well as traveling to Costa Rica, is that the mere act of being here will slowly change you, even without you actively trying to do so. All you have to do is be open to it and take that feeling with you when you go back home.

Since I moved here back in 2018, I have already changed quite a bit. Contrary to my own cultural background, Ticos easily cast away negative thoughts and are so, so laid-back. As a result, I started to feel silly about getting so stressed over the tardiness, flakiness and other traits that also define a large portion of the populace. After a while, it will seem like you are just raging against yourself while everyone else has no idea what on earth you are getting so worked up about.

While I will always be myself and never become either tardy or flaky, I am slowly but surely learning to shrug rather than stress, and allowing the healing presence of sun, nature and friendly people soften some of the edges of, what Allan refers to as, 'my German side'.

# PACKING AND PLANNING TIPS

## A Week before Leaving

- Arrange for someone to take care of pets and water plants.

- Email and Print important Documents.

- Get Visa and vaccines if needed.

- Check for travel warnings.

- Stop mail and newspaper.

- Notify Credit Card companies where you are going.

- Passports and photo identification is up to date.

- Pay bills.

- Copy important items and download travel Apps.

- Start collecting small bills for tips.

- Have post office hold mail while you are away.

- Check weather for the week.

- Car inspected, oil is changed, and tires have the correct pressure.

- Check airline luggage restrictions.

- Download Apps needed for your trip.

## Right Before Leaving

- Contact bank and credit cards to tell them your location.

- Clean out refrigerator.

- Empty garbage cans.

- Lock windows.

- Make sure you have the proper identification with you.

- Bring cash for tips.

- Remember travel documents.

- Lock door behind you.

- Remember wallet.

- Unplug items in house and pack chargers.

- Change your thermostat settings.

- Charge electronics, and prepare camera memory cards.

# READ OTHER GREATER THAN A TOURIST BOOKS

*Greater Than a Tourist- Geneva Switzerland: 50 Travel Tips from a Local* by Amalia Kartika

*Greater Than a Tourist- St. Croix US Birgin Islands USA: 50 Travel Tips from a Local* by Tracy Birdsall

*Greater Than a Tourist- San Juan Puerto Rico: 50 Travel Tips from a Local* by Melissa Tait

*Greater Than a Tourist – Lake George Area New York USA: 50 Travel Tips from a Local* by Janine Hirschklau

*Greater Than a Tourist – Monterey California United States: 50 Travel Tips from a Local* by Katie Begley

*Greater Than a Tourist – Chanai Crete Greece: 50 Travel Tips from a Local* by Dimitra Papagrigoraki

*Greater Than a Tourist — The Garden Route Western Cape Province South Africa: 50 Travel Tips from a Local* by Li-Anne McGregor van Aardt

*Greater Than a Tourist – Sevilla Andalusia Spain: 50 Travel Tips from a Local* by Gabi Gazon

Children's Book: *Charlie the Cavalier Travels the World* by Lisa Rusczyk

# > TOURIST

Follow us on Instagram for beautiful travel images:
http://Instagram.com/GreaterThanATourist

Follow *Greater Than a Tourist* on Amazon.

# > TOURIST

At *Greater Than a Tourist*, we love to share travel tips with you. How did we do? What guidance do you have for how we can give you better advice for your next trip? Please send your feedback to GreaterThanaTourist@gmail.com as we continue to improve the series. We appreciate your constructive feedback. Thank you.

# METRIC CONVERSIONS

## TEMPERATURE

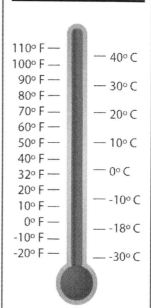

110° F —
100° F —
90° F —   — 40° C
80° F —   — 30° C
70° F —   — 20° C
60° F —
50° F —   — 10° C
40° F —
32° F —   — 0° C
20° F —
10° F —   — -10° C
0° F —    — -18° C
-10° F —
-20° F —  — -30° C

### To convert F to C:
Subtract 32, and then multiply by 5/9 or .5555.

### To Convert C to F:
Multiply by 1.8 and then add 32.

### 32F = 0C

## LIQUID VOLUME

**To Convert:..................Multiply by**
U.S. Gallons to Liters................ 3.8
U.S. Liters to Gallons ................26
Imperial Gallons to U.S. Gallons 1.2
Imperial Gallons to Liters....... 4.55
Liters to Imperial Gallons ........22
**1 Liter = .26 U.S. Gallon**
**1 U.S. Gallon = 3.8 Liters**

## DISTANCE

**To convert ............Multiply by**
Inches to Centimeters ....2.54
Centimeters to Inches ........39
Feet to Meters....................... .3
Meters to Feet ...................3.28
Yards to Meters ...................91
Meters to Yards ...............1.09
Miles to Kilometers .........1.61
Kilometers to Miles............ .62
**1 Mile = 1.6 km**
**1 km = .62 Miles**

## WEIGHT

1 Ounce = .28 Grams
1 Pound = .4555 Kilograms
1 Gram = .04 Ounce
1 Kilogram = 2.2 Pounds

# TRAVEL QUESTIONS

- Do you bring presents home to family or friends after a vacation?

- Do you get motion sick?

- Do you have a favorite billboard?

- Do you know what to do if there is a flat tire?

- Do you like a sun roof open?

- Do you like to eat in the car?

- Do you like to wear sun glasses in the car?

- Do you like toppings on your ice cream?

- Do you use public bathrooms?

- Did you bring your cell phone and does it have power?

- Do you have a form of identification with you?

- Have you ever been pulled over by a cop?

- Have you ever given money to a stranger on a road trip?

- Have you ever taken a road trip with animals?

- Have you ever went on a vacation alone?

- Have you ever run out of gas?

- If you could move to any place in the world, where would it be?

- If you could travel anywhere in the world, where would you travel?

- If you could travel in any vehicle, which one would it be?

- If you had three things to wish for from a magic genie, what would they be?

- If you have a driver's license, how many times did it take you to pass the test?

- What are you the most afraid of on vacation?

- What do you want to get away from the most when you are on vacation?

- What foods smells bad to you?

- What item do you bring on ever trip with you away from home?

- What makes you sleepy?

- What song would you love to hear on the radio when you're cruising on the highway?

- What travel job would you want the least?

- What will you miss most while you are away from home?

- What is something you always wanted to try?

- What is the best road side attraction that you ever saw?

- What is the farthest distance you ever biked?

- What is the farthest distance you ever walked?

- What is the weirdest thing you needed to buy while on vacation?

- What is your favorite candy?

- What is your favorite color car?

- What is your favorite family vacation?

- What is your favorite food?

- What is your favorite gas station drink or food?

- What is your favorite license plate design?

- What is your favorite restaurant?

- What is your favorite smell?

- What is your favorite song?

- What is your favorite sound that nature makes?

- What is your favorite thing to bring home from a vacation?

- What is your favorite vacation with friends?

- What is your favorite way to relax?

- Where is the farthest place you ever traveled in a car?

- Where is the farthest place you ever went North, South, East and West?

- Where is your favorite place in the world?

- Who is your favorite singer?

- Who taught you how to drive?

- Who will you miss the most while you are away?

- Who if the first person you will contact when you get to your destination?

- Who brought you on your first vacation?

- Who likes to travel the most in your life?

- Would you rather be hot or cold?

- Would you rather drive above, below, or at the speed limited?

- Would you rather drive on a highway or a back road?

- Would you rather go on a train or a boat?

- Would you rather go to the beach or the woods?

# TRAVEL BUCKET LIST

1.

2.

3.

4.

5.

6.

7.

8.

9.

10.

# NOTES

65185954R00059

Made in the USA
Middletown, DE
02 September 2019